Striving to Become

a Proverbs 31

Woman

Heidi Lynn

Striving to Become a Proverbs 31 Woman

Copyright © 2018 by Heidi Lynn

ISBN 9781976852060

I want to take a moment to say thank you to the line of amazing, God fearing women that I came from and that have shown me the way to leave a Godly legacy. You all mean so much to me and I can't imagine what my life would have been like without you!

Thank you, and I love you all more than you will ever know.

To: My Mom Sheila, My Grandma Kuiper and My Grandma Mohler

Give grace, Live grace and Love gracefully ~ Heidi Lynn

About Me:

My name is Heidi Lynn, I am a wife to a very dedicated husband who loves me and tolerates all my endless new ideas. A mother to four amazing children who sometimes drive me crazy! They are each perfect in their own way, they make me laugh and I couldn't imagine living without them. I love Jesus, my family, my friends and cheese. Here is my story: I became saved by grace at the age of 12. I went to an event called Acquire the Fire with my youth group and my life was changed. I was raised in a Christian home and was a good kid but at THAT moment I knew that I needed Jesus. With my hands held high and tears in my eyes (and again now as I type these words) I opened my heart and allowed my Lord and Savior to come inside.

A few years later my family moved churches, we went from a large church in the city with a very large youth group to a very small church in the country with a very small youth group. I was angry for a long time that my parents moved me away from all those friends (thankfully I have still been able to hold on to a few of them) and eventually I made new friends. Not only did I make new friends but my friends from school started going with me. My dad became the Pastor of that church in 1999. To this day we still attend this church, 18 years later. Mt. Pleasant Baptist Church has gone through many seasons and many changes but it is home and they are my family now.

Life hasn't always been perfect, I have faced many storms, many battles, and many trials but I have never been left alone. I have made mistakes, I have failed and I have fallen on my face but I have also been forgiven. Sometimes things are very hard and we have no idea how we will ever make it through or what the outcome will be but if we look to the Son we will never have to worry, fret or fear. I serve a big and mighty God and He holds my tomorrow in the eternal grasp of His loving hands. I pray that this book helps draw you a little closer than you already are to the Father who loves YOU, wants YOU and died for YOU.

Father God, use me as your tool to pull on the heart strings of each and every reader that they may come to a closer walk with you. May they find my words honest, real, and true. Let them know that they are not alone and are not the only one striving to become a Proverbs 31 woman. So many of us strive every single day with every fiber of our being. Lord bless each one of them in Your Holy Name, Father. ~Amen

This book is not meant to make you feel bad or discouraged about the woman, wife and mother that you are now. My desire for this book is to give you hope, courage, and knowledge as a daughter of the King. Don't be discouraged, be inspired, and be blessed.

Proverbs 31:10-31 New International Version (NIV)

Epilogue: The Wife of Noble Character

10 A wife of noble character who can find?
   She is worth far more than rubies.
11 Her husband has full confidence in her
   and lacks nothing of value.
12 She brings him good, not harm,
   all the days of her life.
13 She selects wool and flax
   and works with eager hands.
14 She is like the merchant ships,
   bringing her food from afar.
15 She gets up while it is still night;
   she provides food for her family
   and portions for her female servants.
16 She considers a field and buys it;
   out of her earnings she plants a vineyard.
17 She sets about her work vigorously;
   her arms are strong for her tasks.
18 She sees that her trading is profitable,
   and her lamp does not go out at night.

19 In her hand she holds the distaff
   and grasps the spindle with her fingers.
20 She opens her arms to the poor
   and extends her hands to the needy.
21 When it snows, she has no fear for her household;
   for all of them are clothed in scarlet.
22 She makes coverings for her bed;
   she is clothed in fine linen and purple.
23 Her husband is respected at the city gate,
   where he takes his seat among the elders of the land.
24 She makes linen garments and sells them,
   and supplies the merchants with sashes.
25 She is clothed with strength and dignity;
   she can laugh at the days to come.
26 She speaks with wisdom,
   and faithful instruction is on her tongue.

27 She watches over the affairs of her household
   and does not eat the bread of idleness.
28 Her children arise and call her blessed;
   her husband also, and he praises her:
29 "Many women do noble things,
   but you surpass them all."

30 Charm is deceptive, and beauty is fleeting;
   but a woman who fears the Lord is to be praised.
31 Honor her for all that her hands have done,
   and let her works bring her praise at the city gate.

This is one of my FAVORITE passages in the Bible. This woman is *amazing,* but I have to admit… sometimes, most of the time, I have a Proverbs 31 phobia!! Sounds crazy I know, but it's true. Some people look at the Proverbs 31 woman and think "I don't even like her! There is no way that is even possible!" "This woman is too intimidating!" Well guess what!? God isn't calling us to be this woman overnight. Thank goodness, right? We have a lifetime of relying on God and building our relationship with Him so that we can become the Proverbs 31 woman in Him and through Him. There is NO way we will be able to do it on our own.

I am far from the Proverbs 31 woman even though it is truly my heart's desire to be her and I will continue to reach for that goal forever. My faith has always been there but my commitment to God is stronger now than ever before. You can be a Proverbs 31 woman too, it IS going to take some time, there will be A LOT of bumps in the road but we HAVE to rely on God and trust in Him with every single aspect of our lives. God loves you **right where you are right now,** but he doesn't want you to stay there, he has bigger and better things in store for you!

This is not a woman that **we automatically are, this is a woman that we become**. The standards look so high and unattainable but with Christ they are more than attainable.

What is Woman? Woman is made in the image of God because man is the image of God. Woman is made to be man's companion. We are not whole on our own, we are made to complete the man. Genesis 2:18 says The LORD God said, "It is not good for the man to be alone. I will make a helper suitable for him." We are going to look at the characteristics of a Godly woman....

This passage is written by the Queen, and she is a mother giving her son instructions on what he should be looking for in a wife. The woman that she recommends is the woman that intimidates us, but she shouldn't. She shouldn't be the woman that we compare ourselves to but the woman that we strive every single day to become.

10   A wife of noble character who can find?   She is worth far more than rubies.

11   Her husband has full confidence in her and lacks nothing of value.

This woman is RARE. To some people, like my husband, this how you order a steak, but to some people it's like a ruby or a diamond. To my 10 year old son it's every single penny that he finds and has to pick up because he may not find another one anytime soon.   But rare is defined as, "seldom occurring or something that is seldom found", meaning quite simply she is <u>hard to find</u>. She is not to be of the world but unlike the world, set apart and different. We are called to be strong, mighty, and kind   to our husbands and children. Sometimes I feel like I am not doing anything right (I'm sure I'm not the only one that feels this way), and nothing is going as planned. We all have those days, right? Then out of the middle of nowhere there are those little rare moments that are like reminders from God saying, "Hey, you aren't doing too bad after all." One of the moments happened around Christmas time. I had wrapped all the kids' presents except my oldest son's because I didn't have his yet. He was getting ready to leave to go on a vacation with his dad, so I wanted to get his presents wrapped and under the tree before he left. I did just that, and I said, "Hey Buddy, you finally have presents under the tree." He caught me off guard when he looked up at me and said, "Mom I'd be fine with even just one present because that's not what Christmas is about, and some kids don't even get one." In that moment he made my heart smile. To me that was one of those rare moments from God saying, "See you ARE doing something right."

We have to have a DEEP RELATIONSHIP with God to understand when he is speaking to us. A deep relationship means not to just know that I am Heidi... people know that I am a photographer, a mother, and a wife, but many of those people don't know me on a personal level. If you know me on a personal level you know that I HATE pickles, I LOVE to talk, and I LOVE my family, and my mother is one of very best friends. I love scrapbooking, painting, Bible journaling, and so much more. But if you don't have a personal relationship with me you probably don't know these things. That's how a relationship is with God; it has to be personal, intimate, and deep. Which means we have to love, trust, and confide in Him daily. When God speaks to us, He speaks in many different ways. He can speak to us through circumstances, the Bible, through Christian friends and other ways, but when we have that deep relationship with God we KNOW when he is speaking to us. We know when it really is Him and don't have to doubt or fear. The Proverbs 31 woman loves God with her whole heart and she relies on Him. She and her husband are also a team, and they trust each other in everything. He trusts her with his children, his finances and his life. He has full confidence in her knowing that she is doing the very best that she can. He lifts her up and supports her daily. I can not thank my husband enough for letting me be the things that I want to be and to do the things that I want to do. He almost always fully supports me. Now there are many times he makes me take a step back and think first, but sometimes I need that voice of reason or I would jump in feet first at the drop of a hat when that may not be the best thing for our family.

Now let's take a minute to reflect, do you have a deep relationship with God, or even a relationship for that matter? Is it one sided or are you letting Him lead the way? Ask God right now to come close and speak to you in a way in that undeniable voice of God. Be ready; be prepared because this relationship is more important than any other!

12   She brings him good, not harm, all the days of her life

She is there for her husband all the days of her life. This means through good, bad, happy, sad, angry, and yes, through sickness and health. The divorce rate shows that 50% of all marriages end in divorce. Now it also shows that the older people are when they get married the lower the rate is. I understand that there are many things in life that may not go the way we plan, and part of the problem is that it shouldn't be our plan to begin with. It should be God's plan. I am here today to tell you that I am a statistic in both ways. I was divorced at the age of 21, and I have also now been remarried for 13 years. I am married to my husband through sickness and health ALL the days of our lives, and trust me that health one has definitely been tested many times over the years. Not only have I struggled with many different health issues off and on of my own (thankfully none too serious), but my husband has a heart condition and is disabled. He had a major heart episode a year ago that stopped us dead in our tracks. The outcome could have been so much worse than it was, and I will forever be grateful for the emergency crew on staff that day. I will never forget the feeling I felt standing at my husband's feet in that room, helpless, and so afraid but you know what… God ALWAYS provides and by the grace of God we have come this far, grown so much stronger than we were before and more than we ever imagined being.

Now let's a take a minute to reflect, life throws curveballs more than we ever care to imagine, but we have to know to lean on each other in love and support. Above all we must lean on the Everlasting Father. Are you leaning on His everlasting arms today?

13   She selects wool and flax and works with eager hands.

14   She is like the merchant ships bringing her food from afar.

Now back to this woman: we are supposed to be a woman that is HUMBLE and that is WILLING to work, work with our hands and provide in whatever way that is needed for our family. Trust me, sometimes there are major life changes, and you don't have a choice, this woman will step up and provide for her loved ones. This can be a job outside of the home or inside. It doesn't matter how we provide for them but that we do. Sometimes we are overwhelmed with the weekly and daily tasks that we have to do such as dishes, laundry, cooking and cleaning but it is actually noble to do these things. God is honored when we do these things eagerly without dread and complaint. 1 Corinthians 10:10 says, do not grumble as some of them did, and were killed by the destroying angel. I don't know about you, but that is scary! We should never complain against God! We should not complain against the blessing or tasks that God has given us. Complaining against God is a **SIN**. Just imagine how our lives would be if no one wanted or was willing to do the laundry or to cook dinner. Our lives would be a disaster, and not only that but what kind of example would that be for our children? Instead, we should be thanking God that we HAVE laundry to fold and food to cook and that we ARE able to provide for our family! My children are old enough now that they have started to help out with the daily chores. Actually, they do most of the chores. And yes, I do come home from working all day and get frustrated because things aren't done that should be done, but they are children, and while I believe that it is good for them to learn these responsibilities, they sometimes forget things too, and I need to remind myself of that. Not one of us is perfect and things will never be done perfectly. Sometimes we just have to go with the flow. Sometimes it's not worth it to make them re-stack the towels that aren't perfectly in their place. It is ok to say, "It's not worth it today, at least they tried."

Verse 14 in modern days to me means that we are willing to SEARCH OUT and get HEALTHY foods or to try new recipes and make things that are better for our families, not always running to the store and grabbing chicken nuggets and pizza rolls, but actually taking the time to cook a wholesome meal. Oh, trust me, I am a big fan of ordering pizza or "fend for yourself nights", but we simply cannot do this all the time or our children and families will not receive the nutrition that they need. I am NOT a health nut at all, but I am working on getting better at this; however, I do cook homemade meals most nights because this is what my family needs, and that's what works for us. I am NOT saying there is anything wrong with take out and easy dinners, sometimes that alone helps save our sanity. Sometimes I come home and my husband has dinner ready to go and my heart smiles so big thinking that 1) I didn't have to cook, 2) my children see that their father is also able to provide for them in this way, and 3) we get different meals than the ones that I feel like I get stuck in a rut of making over and over again. Thankfully, my husband is a really good cook, so it's an even better treat for all of us! He's welcome to cook everyday if he would like! Every family operates differently, and I get that, and that's ok. I'm not saying that our way is the only way, but taking the time to cook, prepare, and serve your family meals will show them how much you love and care for their well-being. Another way to feed your children is to feed them spiritually. We must feed them the Word of God so they know how to live their lives in accordance to His design. I truly believe that spiritually feeding our family is just as important as physically feeding them.

Now let's take a minute to reflect, what are some ways that you could be providing for your family that you aren't already doing? Are you raising your children up the way they should go? Proverbs 22:6 says: Start children off on the way they should go, and even when they are old they will not turn from it. Take some time to honor God by doing the things that we normally want to grumble and complain about. Try something new that you haven't done before; mix it up, and see how you are blessed by a new mindset.

15   She gets up while it is still night; she provides food for her family and portions for her female servants.

Now the first part of this verse says, "She gets up while it's still dark..." Oh boy that's a tough one for me! I used to stay up really late and do my editing for my photography business while the kids were in bed and I didn't have any running to do. By late I mean midnight to 2:00 in the morning most nights. Now it was easy for me get up, get the kids ready, and take them to school, but then I would come back home and go right back to bed. My day typically didn't really get going until about 10:00 a.m. or later... So this was a really big struggle for me. We get stuck in these habits and it's really hard to break them. Sometimes I would get myself on more of a "normal" schedule, but I always slowly drifted back to my really late nights. This all changed for me two years ago and my world was turned upside down in a positive way. A great job opportunity landed in my lap that I hadn't really expected or been searching for. I panicked a lot because it was an 8-5 job that I hadn't had in YEARS, and honestly I hated 8-5 jobs. I just thought they weren't for me, and I knew that it would be a big adjustment. I had been doing my own thing with no boss and no one to report to for years. I could take the kids to appointments whenever I needed to. Then that all changed, I am now on someone else's schedule. But you know what? I wouldn't change it for the world! I have BECOME more of a morning person. I CHOOSE to make each morning positive, (even though they don't always start out that way, literally this morning I was late to work because I had to get dried gum out of my daughter's hair)! At work I once stated that I was NOT a morning person at all, and they were shocked, but coming to a job that you love makes a huge difference. I love the team of people that I work with and our mission, which makes it perfect for me. Now these situations are different for everyone, you know. If you've recently had a baby, your sleep schedule will revolve around the baby,

and you will probably need to sleep in in the morning, but that's ok! What we are really looking at here is this woman rises and gets her house ready for daily tasks and takes responsibility. This is also a perfect time to spend time with God if you are up early before anyone else and before any distractions of the day have emerged. You can take this time for your daily devotion and prayer time with God to prepare yourself for the day ahead. Starting out with God also helps you keep a focus on Him throughout the day. I have to admit, I am more of a night time devotion person, but you have to find what works for you. You have a cell phone don't you? Well, I have to charge my cell phone EVERY SINGLE DAY because if I don't, guess what!? The power goes dead! It's the same way with God's Word. We NEED to plug in daily so we are filled with Him and His mindset. Doing this everyday is going to change you, keep you spiritually grounded and will keep us on track with Him. The distractions will become minimal, and we will become fully aware of God's presence in our lives. The distractions will become minimal, and we will become fully aware of God's presence in our lives.

Next we are talking about food again, and it is obviously very important to provide food for our families. Again, this woman seeks good food and nutrition for them. Now trust me, I know this isn't always easy, I have a VERY picky 8 year old who would LOVE to only eat chicken nuggets and pizza rolls every day! However, it is VERY important for me to get him to try new things and not to give in to letting him have what he wants. When he was younger we figured out that he doesn't like his food to touch or to be mixed up, so if I could I would separate things for him to an extent, but he was required to try at least one bite of the meal the same way everyone else was eating it. Believe it or not we don't have nearly as many meltdowns, and

22

he is trying new things, and sometimes he even likes them! He really has come a long way and eats so many more things. What would have happened if I would have just given in and let him eat something completely different? I would be making two meals every single night, and that wouldn't be teaching him anything. I am not talking about kids with allergies, serious taste aversions, or medical issues here, I am just talking about making sure that their needs are met, and that they are trying new things and broadening their horizons. We have to be willing to provide the food and nutrition that our families need; it is our responsibility to our families and to God. Not only are we providing the food, but also meal times are a great time to fellowship with our husbands and our children. I have SO many memories of sitting at the dinner table talking about my day. Sometimes I can't believe that my parents ever even asked me day after day how my day was, because then they got stuck there for what seemed like hours, now that I look back on it. But those memories mean SO much to me, and I know my parents really cared and really wanted to know what was going on in my life. They were probably even a little entertained! I want that same thing for my children, and meal time is one time that we are sitting in the same area for more than 5 minutes. I challenge you to take that time to make sure you eat at the table together, pray together, and ask your children how their day was. You WILL be blessed and they will KNOW that you care.

Portions for her servant girls means that even though the servants job was to care for the family, a wife and mother's job is make sure that everyone, including the servant, is getting their needs met. She did not leave them out because they are an important part of the home also.

Now let's take a minute to reflect: are you rising and preparing your family for the day ahead? Are you preparing your heart for the day ahead? Find a time that works for you to be in solitude and communicate with God. Let Him help you prepare for the day ahead. Let Him charge you with His strength, love, and mercy. Take time to invest in your family, whether it be at mealtime, bedtime or any other time. Just take time, make time to invest in them and your family unit as a whole.

16   She considers a field and buys it; out of her earnings she plants a vineyard.

What do we see in verse 16? The first thing that we see is that she considers the field. She doesn't irrationally buy; it she takes the time to think about it and to pray about it. She is wise and responsible with her money. Then after she buys it, what does she do with it? It doesn't just sit there untouched so she can look at it, she works in it. She takes her earnings and plants a vineyard. This woman is a HARD WORKER, isn't she? Sometimes it's hard to make wise choices when we make purchases. I will see this cute little outfit and I HAVE to get it, but does Tori really need it? NO! I have horrible buyer's remorse. I will carry things through the store that I am planning on buying, but by the time I'm ready to checkout I have talked myself out of most, if not all, of the things that I didn't need to begin with. Sometimes (more than I would like to admit) I even purchase things and then take them back because I didn't really need them. We are called to be <u>wise</u> and <u>responsible</u> with our money. This also includes our <u>tithing</u> and giving our money back to God. We must be thankful for having it to begin with. Malachi 3:8-12 says 8 "Will a man rob God? Yet you are robbing Me! But you say, 'How have we robbed You?' In tithes and offerings. 9 "You are cursed with a curse, for you are robbing Me, the whole nation *of you!* 10 "Bring the whole tithe into the storehouse, so that there may be food in My house, and test Me now in this," says the LORD of hosts, "if I will not open for you the windows of heaven and pour out for you a blessing until it overflows. 11 "Then I will rebuke the devourer for you, so that it will not destroy the fruits of the ground; nor will your vine in the field cast *its grapes,*" says the LORD of hosts. 12 "All the nations will call you blessed, for you shall be a delightful land," says the LORD of hosts. And, 2 Corinthians 9:7 says each of you should give what you have decided in your heart to give, not reluctantly or under compulsion, for God loves a cheerful giver. That's sounds very scary to me, who wants to rob God? I sure don't, and honestly this is a place that I struggle. It's not an intentional struggle but something that I have to remind myself about and be conscious and aware that I am called to give back to God because he has graciously given to me.

Now let's take a minute to reflect, are you an irrational spender? Ask God to help you and guide you. The more you rely on Him, the more you are conscious of His presence in your decision making process. This goes for all decision making, not just when you are purchasing something. Ask God to help you take your earnings and plant a vineyard. Then be prepared to give back to Him because He will help you and provide for you.

17   She sets about her work vigorously; her arms are strong for her tasks.

In verse 17 we see that she works vigorously, which is defined as: Done with great force or energy, meaning she works hard to accomplish the task at hand. She doesn't get to the middle and say, "oh my goodness this is too difficult" and give up, but she continues to work and to work hard to complete it. It is very important for women to spend time IN our homes home-making. We all know how it is when we take a day off from daily task. Things begin to slowly spiral out of control. We need to take the time to diligently work at home as a wife and mother because it is a responsibility to manage the home. Now, that doesn't mean things outside the home aren't important, but home is a foundation for our children's lives and it is where they are being shaped and molded for their future. They grow in so many different ways: physically, emotionally and spiritually throughout the time that we have them in our homes. Our husbands and our children need us there to be Godly and Christ like because they spend so much time out IN THE WORLD. Being those things will keep our family grounded in faith and comforted in their own home. This does not mean our homes have to be perfectly clean and spotless and that we have to cook and clean the whole time that we are there. None of us live in a perfect home, and none of us ever will. We have to do what needs to be done, but we also have to take time to be WITH our family and to build those foundations. Take a break, be with them, and go do things with them. Maybe you have children and family that are grown, so these things look a little different for you, but you can still take time and pray for them or invite them into your home just to be with them. Show them that even though they don't live with you, the foundation of "home" is still there and is still very important.

Now let's take a minute to reflect. It is very important to work diligently in our homes. I know it's exhausting, trust me, but there are things that just need to be done. We need to also be that model for our children so they are prepared when they move on to this season of their life. Make sure you take a break, though. Take time to be with your family, and take time for yourself. You cannot function if you are exhausted from housework all the time. Not only that, but when we are exhausted, we become frustrated, which then send signals that we may not intend to send. Ask God to help you work vigorously and gratefully.

18   She sees that her trading is profitable, and her lamp does not go out at night.

In 18 we see that she sees that her trade is profitable, meaning whatever she is selling she is smart about it and makes enough profit to put back into her finances. This woman is a business woman. She continues to be available through the night and knows that her hard work is paying off and is necessary. We have to look at the reality of the Proverbs 31 woman, she had no television, nothing to stay up and watch, and no radio to listen to. So her "late at night" could have been 9:00 p.m., well after it was dark outside. The fact of the matter is that we have TV, radio, lights, computers, phones with games, and all kinds of <u>false</u> daylights that keep us up at night when what we really should be doing is <u>resting</u> and <u>preparing</u> for the next day. Her lamp not going out at night makes me think of my children, sometimes. Actually, a lot of times. They need us in the middle of the night, and we need to be rested and ready to handle a situation with love and grace, not anger and shortness because we were awakened at 4:30 a.m. I can't tell you how many times I woke my parents up in the night (I was a bit of a baby), but never was I yelled at or sent back to bed. I was always welcomed with loving arms. Eventually, I just took my pillow and blanket and went and slept on their floor because I knew that it was ok for me to be there. Like I said earlier, I used to go to bed late and sleep in late, now I get to bed closer to "on time" and I get up much earlier, but my children were, and are ALWAYS, welcome and able to come to me in the middle of the night, no matter what the issue is. I can't say that I always love getting awakened in the middle of the night, and I can't say that I have always been in the best mood when they need me, but I try my hardest to be there and to show love and grace.

So, over and over we are looking at this woman's work ethic. This is a Godly woman who is willing to work for God, her husband, and her family. Let me say that again....this is a Godly woman that is willing to work for God, <u>her husband, and her family.</u>

Now let's take a minute to reflect. Not everyone is able to work like this woman, and sometimes we can't work at all, but there is one thing that you always do no matter what, PRAY! Ask God to show you what you can do for your family? He will show you. Be available for your children and your family when they need you, not when you are ready for them. This will mean the world to them when they are grown. Don't let your lamp go out at night.

19   In her hand she holds the distaff and grasps the spindle with her fingers.

20   She opens her arms to the poor and extends her hands to the needy.

So far we see that this woman's whole life is focused on the Lord, and that's how she gets her strength and energy, through her relationship WITH God. We've also looked at her relationship with her husband and with her children, and now it is time to look at her relationship with others. In verse 19 she works with the tools that she has at hand. And in 20 she opens her arms to the poor and needy. She isn't too busy with her every day life to take time and notice others in need. Then she takes action and does something about it. Sometimes we get so wrapped up in so many things that we don't even take the time to stop and see someone in need. I wonder how many people and how many opportunities we pass by because we simply aren't paying attention. Many times I find myself praying to God, "please show me someone in need today. Someone who needs a helping hand, an ear to listen or even just a smile. Let me be Jesus to someone today." And you would not believe what happens, it happens! I find myself right in the middle of a situation where I can be of help to someone who I may not have even noticed if I hadn't asked God to open my eyes and heart that day. We HAVE to watch and be READY to serve others and in return serve God. If we don't do it who will?   Mark 12:30-31 says, "Love the Lord your God with all your heart and with all your soul and with all your mind and with all your strength. The second is this: Love your neighbor as yourself. There is no commandment greater than these."   We are called to love and serve others, now is this always easy? No way, but if we take the time to GENUINELY seek these opportunities we will be BLESSED in ways we can't imagine.

Now let's take a minute to reflect. We need to be the hands and of feet of Jesus to the needy, the poor, the lost, and even to the saved. Everyone needs to see Jesus daily. Even if they only see him through a smile, you may be the only one that smiled at them that day, and it is one of the simplest of gestures. Ask God to show you today someone that needs to see more of Him. Take time to notice and be the light in this cold dark world.

21   When it snows, she has no fear for her household; for all of them are clothed in scarlet.

22   She makes coverings for her bed; she is clothed in fine linen and purple.

We see here that when there is a change in seasons, this woman is not afraid for her household. She knows that they are clothed and have what they need for the changing weather or situations. She is PREPARED, thinks ahead, and is not <u>caught off guard</u>. It is very important for us as moms to shop ahead of time and prepare. I love to watch for deals when I am shopping ahead. I am not a fan of paying full price for clothes, but I still want my children to have the quality that they need. So, I really do try to buy ahead and not buy irrationally. Now there are times when my son tries on his jeans and they are two inches too small because finally he grew for the first time in years, but that's when you take the time to buy the necessary things that you need. Shopping really is a good thing as long as we are doing it correctly and buying what our family really needs. On the other side of this, we should be willing to donate items that we no longer need because someone may be in a greater need than we are. You never know what type of season someone is going through. If you are in a place where you can help others, please do it! I have been there before, and I have needed help, so I feel like I am giving back when I am able to donate bags of clothing or even just passing them along to my friends who have smaller children. People appreciate this help so much more than we know. We see that they were clothed in scarlet, which means they are expensive and the quality was high, but we also see that earlier in the verses she was working hard and making that profit, so she is able to provide for the needs of her family.

In 22 we see that she makes coverings for her beds. She pays attention to the place that her family sleeps because they are important to her. It is also our job to make sure that our children have a clean place to sleep and a comfortable place to rest. Now, she was actually making the coverings for their beds, and I am not talented in that way, but I can at least make sure my kids have a clean warm place to sleep. She also could not run to Wal-Mart to get new sheets when they were needed, so she had to provide for her family in this way. This shows us that EVERY area of their lives is important to her, from the clothes they wear for the day to where they lay their head at night.

Then we see that she, herself, is clothed in fine linen and purple. After she has taken care of everyone else's needs, that's when we see that she worries about herself. She is sacrificing for her family, but when she gets to herself she still takes care of herself and dresses appropriately. Dressing ourselves varies widely from person. Some women love to dress up and some women love to be artistic with their clothes. Me? I LOVE my jeans and t-shirts. That is what I am most comfortable in and what I accomplish the most in; however, there are times I like to dress up, but when I shop for myself I shop the same way I shop for my kids. I have absolutely no problem with buying quality clothes off the clearance rack. For me this is what works, and I can dress nicely but be financially responsible for my family. When I got the job that I told you about earlier, I was in no way prepared for the attire that I would need to wear. Yes, I had Sunday dresses that I wore to church, but I had a very limited amount because 8 dresses would get you through two months of church before having to wear them again, am I right!? Obviously I needed more dress clothes than that for my new job, which included slacks that I had none of. I had two pairs of black dress shoes and two pairs of brown dress shoes, and that was it for shoes. There was this great sale though, right after I started working, on dress shoes, so I told my husband I needed to go get some. We went shopping, and I didn't expect to fall in love with all the pretty colors! I bought six pairs of dress shoes in ONE DAY! The best part was that they were only $10 a pair! Two years later I am still wearing those shoes; to me that's a great investment! Along with the shoes, I slowly started building my dress attire. I didn't go crazy all at once, I just bought a couple of things at a time (usually when they were on sale), and now I have a wide variety of dress clothes. Every situation and woman is different. You have to do what works for you, for your family, and for the glory of God. So, just remember that it's ok to shop, but shop responsibly and stay within your family's budget. The Proverbs 31 woman never put her family in financial strain because of her shopping; she shopped wisely and for what was necessary.

Now let's take a minute to reflect. Are you preparing your family for what is to come? The changing seasons in our lives will determine the needs that we have, but when we are prepared we usually feel better and less stressed. Make sure that your family has what they need for the future when that is an option. But also make sure to take time to take care of yourself; you must also be a priority. Don't only take care of yourself physical but spiritually. Ask God to help you know the difference between necessary and unnecessary, if that is something that you struggle with. He will prepare you for the future.

23   Her husband is respected at the city gate, where he takes his seat among the elders of the land.

24   She makes linen garments and sells them, and supplies the merchants with sashes.

25   She is clothed with strength and dignity; she can laugh at the days to come.

     The Proverbs 31 woman is an enabler in a good way. She allows her husband to work outside of the home and to be respected in the land. We see here that he is also respected because he sits with the elders. It is important for our husband to learn and to grow in wisdom also, because of their partnership they work well together inside the home and outside the home. Now she is making and selling garments, which is yet another form of income. We also see that she works with many different types of people and works successfully with them. Just imagine how this woman is influencing ALL these different types of people and influencing them in a positive way. That is TRULY my heart's desire: to be a positive influence to everyone I meet. I have bad days too, BUT it's how we handle those people and those circumstances that leave a lasting impression. I strive to handle situations with grace and dignity as I believe the Proverbs 31 women would.

     I love this part of the scripture in verse 25 where we see that she is clothed with strength and dignity and she can laugh at the days to come. Think about this, the most valuable parts of our wardrobe do not hang on the hangers in our closets. This strength is one of the mind, heart, and soul because of a foundation with God. She is clothed with this strength. This dignity means honor, beauty, and excellence that she is clothed in because of her foundation with God. She has a confidence that comes from this deep relationship. She carries herself in a manner of strength and dignity and is <u>confident,</u> but she is <u>not conceited and arrogant</u>, she is a humble and God-fearing woman. She knows that the Lord loves her and she trusts him with EVERY aspect of her life. She can laugh at the days to come because she knows that God holds her future in His hands and that her future is bright and that good is coming. Even if she is going through struggles or is in the middle of a storm, she knows that God is right there with her and will carry her through to a better tomorrow.

Now let's take a minute to reflect. Are you allowing your husband to be respected and enabling him to grow in the grace and wisdom of God or are you holding him back? Encourage him to seek wisdom from mature Christians around him and from God. Are you clothed in strength and dignity today? Humble yourself before the Lord and allow Him to clothe you with His characteristics, not our own. Ask Him to help you become humble and God fearing.

26   **She speaks with wisdom, and faithful**

instruction is on her tongue.

    The Proverbs 31 woman did not neglect her mind. She filled it with the wisdom of God's Word. James 1:5 says if any of you lacks wisdom, you should ask God, who gives generously to all without finding fault, and it will be given to you. And Ephesians 1:8 says that he lavished on us. With all wisdom and understanding, she sought out wisdom through God's word. We can also gain wisdom through other people and learning from our elders, those that are wiser or have more years than we; however, we have to be careful what we take in because what we put out, whether it's our words or our actions, is directly reflected by what we take in. If we focus on things of the world: TV, movies, books, music, even friends, and people, then that is what is GOING to come out. And ladies, <u>our speech should be **totally** and **completely** different than the world's speech.</u> I can NOT express that enough, so I'll say it again! OUR SPEECH SHOULD BE TOTALLY AND COMPLETELY DIFFERENT THAN THE WORLD'S SPEECH. (Proverbs 10:19 says sin is not ended by multiplying words, but the prudent hold their tongues.) Not ONLY are the words we use important, but how we speak to our husbands, our children, and those around us is important too. As you know, I was raised in a Christian home. I have never in my entire life heard my parents say a cuss word or take the Lord's name in vain. Thankfully those words are not in my vocabulary either, and my children will NEVER hear those words come from my mouth. I believe this is very important, and I know not everyone was raised like that, and trust me, I know how rare that is, but challenge yourself to speak more Godly at home, with your friends, in your workplace, and on social media. You will be blessed because of it. This Proverbs 31 woman also speaks with faithful instruction, and she was able to give faithful instruction because she is wise. The King James version says in her tongue is the law of kindness. How awesome would that be for someone to describe your tongue that way? (Psalm 34:13 says keep your tongue from evil and your lips from telling lies. Psalm 39:1 says for the director of music. For Jeduthun. A psalm of David. I said, "I will watch my ways and keep my tongue from sin; I will put a muzzle on my mouth while in the presence of the wicked." and Psalm 51:14 says Deliver me from the guilt of bloodshed, O God, you who are God my Savior, and my tongue will sing of your righteousness. This woman had a filter on her tongue. She did not put out anything that wasn't filled with grace and mercy. She controlled her tongue and only gave faithful instruction. We as mothers MUST live this as an example for our children so they then know how to live their lives. Sometimes we need to do this for our husbands also.

Now let's take a minute to reflect. What is coming out of your mouth when you speak? Are they the words that you would want others to hear? If you have no control but need help controlling your tongue, ask God for strength and to help you be aware of when you say things that you shouldn't. Watch the people around you. Are they being a positive influence or are they bringing you down? The more time you spend filling your mind with heavenly instead of worldly things the more positive your tongue will be. Don't let others bring you down, God will help you stand firm.

27   She watches over the affairs of her household and does not eat the bread of idleness.

In verse 27 we see that she is well aware of what goes on in her home. Even though she is a very busy and hardworking woman, she knows what's going on inside of her household. She knows who has ball practice and at what time, she is probably also the one driving them there and home. She knows where her children are and where her husband is because they have spent quality time together and have a strong relationship built on faith and a commitment to one another. One of the ways this can be addressed is at dinner time or whatever mealtime everyone is available. This will not look the same in every household. Again, take time to find out how their day was, what good things happened today or what negative things happened today? Doing this WILL help build a strong relationship with your children. They are never too young to start this, and they are also never too old to start. If you aren't doing this, I beg you start NOW. It may not be easy at first but it will SO be worth it. Also, if you have teenage children, and they have cell phones, have them leave them in their rooms or away from the table so they are not distracted from the moment but are in it with you. This is one of the things that I am really working on, my phone is on me at all times most of the time. I don't even know why because I really don't even like my phone. I have gotten so used to it being a part of my everyday wardrobe that I feel like something is missing without it, or that I will miss out on something, so I have intentionally been leaving my phone away from the table. I leave it in the living room or even on the counter (now sometimes I forget and it is in my pocket), but my phone is NOT important in that moment. My husband and my children deserve my undivided attention, just as later in life I will require theirs. These conversation at the table are a perfect way to find out who is struggling with what or what they have accomplished that day, and it really is necessary for us as mothers to know what is going on and what they are going through. Our culture is so busy and so distracted these days that we <u>have to take time to slow down and focus on our family.</u> We only get one shot in life, so please don't regret it by missing out or being distracted.

When the Proverbs 31 woman took time for herself she didn't allow her <u>eyes</u> to wander away from <u>God</u>. We need to spend our time wisely. What are we reading, watching on TV, what are we discussing with our friends, what songs are we listening too? I'm telling you right now if you listen to a lot of music, find a Christian radio station! I cannot even begin to explain what this does for me. I can become so frustrated or irritated and hop in the car and I hear "You are beautiful my sweet sweet song....." and at that moment realize I am not focusing on God, I am focusing on worldly things and that will get me nowhere. My radio is never on a secular station. If you get in my car you will hear life 88.5 or KLOVE. I NEED that! That music keeps me going that keeps my eyes and my heart focused on God. I am in the car A LOT, and God speaks to me through so many songs. The same goes with the television. Be so very careful what you watch. Our minds can so quickly be distracted. I very rarely watch TV, I just feel like there is nothing worth watching. We actually moved our living room to the basement, and I LOVE IT because I don't have to hear what just seems like pointless noise to me and again it gives me a chance to listen to music. Luke 6:45 says a good man brings good things out of the good stored up in his heart, and an evil man brings evil things out of the evil stored up in his heart. For the mouth speaks what the heart is full of. One time when I was a teenager.... I am not sure my parents know this but.... I took all my secular CDs out to my dad's garage and broke every single one! Like in multiple pieces! To me this was what was going in but not what I wanted to come out. Never once did I miss any of those CDs. Never once did I repurchase any of those CDs. Honestly, I can't even tell you what CDs they were. But it was very important to me to do this, and I really felt like a weight was lifted immediately afterwards. Now I'm not asking you to go and break all your CDs or throw away your movies, but please be conscious about what you ARE watching and listening to and be aware of how it affects your life, and more importantly your <u>children's lives</u>. If breaking or throwing away your secular is what you need to do, then by all means just do it! You won't be disappointed! That kind of went in a little different direction than I planned, but in other words be careful in your down time and keep your eyes focused on God in these times of rest and not on worldly things. I promise you, your family, your kids, other people's kids and your friends ARE watching YOU. What kind of witness are you being to them?

Now let's take a minute to reflect. Do you know what's going on in your household? Take time to build those strong relationships with your children. Try very hard to start getting a routine of meeting together, where you can give them your undivided attention. Ask God to help you find a time that works for everyone. And make sure you are filling yourself with Godly things so that is what is in return coming out. Do not become bored and idle and allow your mind, eyes, and heart to wander. Ask God to help you keep your eyes on Him.

28   Her children arise and call her blessed; her husband also, and he praises her:

29   "Many women do noble things, but you surpass them all."

These verses show that when the Proverbs 31 woman's children have grown, they arise and they call her blessed. They acknowledge her <u>persistent</u> walk with God and her <u>dedication</u> to her husband and family, and they called her <u>blessed</u>. If we are getting our praise only from other people and not from our family at home, then we really need to take time and reflect and make sure we aren't neglecting anything. Who we are at home is who we really are, and we need to be listening to our husbands and children and loving them. Now again, we are not <u>perfect,</u> but we are <u>forgiven,</u> and every day is a new day with new challenges. However, we should always strive for perfect and not settle with the way things are. God has called us be to be so much more. It is also important that we have a Godly husband who recognizes our actions. If our husband and children are not Godly, then we cannot expect them to call us blessed because they simply don't understand the principles. In this verse the husband says, "Many women do noble things but you surpass them all" **WOW,** what a compliment from a husband! How many of us want our husband to say that about us!? I know I do! But we cannot and will not accomplish this overnight. This cannot be accomplished without walking with God. We must know that ultimately we are walking with Him and HE will call us blessed.

Now let's take a minute to reflect. Are you perfect? No? Neither am I, but I am forgiven. I will continue to strive <u>every day</u> to earn the title <u>blessed.</u> I know most of the time it's easier to be one way in public and then let your guard down at home, but sometimes when we stress we are not handling things in a Godly manner. Ask God to help you deal with the stress of the world and to continue to be a Godly example at home. So that one day you will be called <u>blessed.</u>

30   Charm is deceptive, and beauty is fleeting; but a woman who fears the LORD is to be praised.

This verse tells us that we cannot put our self-worth into how we look. Yes, it's nice to dress up and to look beautiful but beauty is fleeting. We will never get any younger than we are today. Another verse that I love is.... Psalm 139:14: "I praise you because I am fearfully and wonderfully made; your works are wonderful, I know that full well." Do you REALLY know that? God made EACH and EVERY ONE of us perfect and we should praise Him for that.

Does that mean that we can't look presentable? NO, it just means that what's on the outside doesn't matter. It's the beauty that's in our heart that counts. This day and age people try to prolong the inevitable by using facial creams or injections and so on, but it really is serving no purpose because natural aging is more beautiful than aging that has been tampered with. I'm not saying it's not ok to take good care of your skin and your body because we are also supposed to take care of our bodies, they are temples for the Lord. To be honest, if you know me very well you know that getting older is something that I really struggle with; however, it is not at all based on my looks. I feel like the older I get the faster time goes, and the minutes, hours, days, months and years seem to slip away so quickly that it really makes me sad sometimes. So, I really have to tell myself OFTEN that God is in control and every moment is precious, not just the ones that have passed, but the ones now and the ones that will come. We WILL get older, and our children WILL get older. It HAS to happen because God has a plan and knows our future. In Jeremiah 29:11 it says, "For I know the plans I have for you, Declares the Lord. Plans to prosper you and not to harm you, plans to give you hope and a future." See? He's got it under control. So, we need to grow old with God and invest in our beauty on the inside. I have a daughter, a beautiful 8 year old daughter and as she grows up it is very important to me that she learns that her true beauty is on the inside. Yes, she had beautiful hair like Rapunzel's before cutting it short, but true beauty is in her heart and people will see that. I promise to teach her that beauty is fleeting and to fear the Lord.

This woman fears the Lord. Fear in this sense is NOT a bad thing. Fearing the Lord is having RESPECT for him and knowing that He is with you and He is in control of every moment of our lives. This makes me think of when I was younger, well even now as an adult, a lot of you know how much I value every opinion of my dad's, but as I was growing up I used to think that I was scared of him, when he said no the answer was no and you can bet that I was in no way going to test that and try to get away with something. As got I older I realized that I was never scared of him, I RESPECTED him and his decisions. He always had my best interest at heart; I knew that and still do. I wanted to honor him and to make him proud, and I HATED to get in trouble, so I respected his authority. That's the way it should be with God. We should fear the Lord in a manner of respect. I mean come on, He deserves that and SO much more. We should live our lives in a way that is honoring to Him and that pleases Him.

Now let's take a minute to reflect. You are beautiful, did you know that? On the inside and the out. God designed you in His image and loves you the way you are. Our bodies are temples, are you taking care of your temple? If not, God can help you if you reach out to Him for strength and guidance. He created you for a purpose. Fear the Lord and honor Him.

31   **Give her the reward she has earned, and let her works bring her praise at the city gate.**

Give her the praise that she deserves. Not the praise she desires, but the praise she earns because she fears the Lord. Think about the rewards that we store up in Heaven, not earthly rewards because they are temporary and will fade just as everything else in this earthly life. Our rewards in Heaven are true and eternal as is our home with the LORD.

Now let's take a minute to reflect. When we get to Heaven our eternal home will be great and beautiful, far beyond anything we can imagine, and we will live forever with the Lord as long as He is our Lord and Savior and lives in our hearts. Is He your Lord and Savior today? If not, ask Him to come into your heart, to forgive you of your sins and to make you a new person through Him. Recognize that Jesus rose from the dead so that YOU could have eternal life.

Wow, we see that this woman is amazing! She works with her hands, she is busy, busy, busy, loves and honors her family, helps the needy and fears the Lord. She does not seek worldly things but Godly things inside her home and in her everyday life. Her love flows out, and everyone that knows her sees her faith in God. Again, we are NOT going to be perfect, but if we work on one area at a time we WILL become more and more like her. As long as I live I will continue to strive to follow in her footsteps, I will continue to strive to become a Proverbs 31 woman.

Now let's take some time to be honest before God. Has God talked to you about any one of these points? Your relationship with God, loving and honoring your husband, providing for your household, working diligently in and out of the home, being a positive role model for your children and everyone around you, your words and/or your actions, or just simply knowing that you CAN do any of these things with the Lord's help and strength?

If you need to start building a relationship with God, you have to do this, I can't do this for you, but I can help guide you. Pray this after me.... Dear God, I want to build a relationship with you, forgive me for living my life my own way and come into my heart and life and be my Lord.....

Father God, I thank you so much for giving me the words to place on these pages. I pray that they may pierce the heart of the woman reading this and that these words help draw her closer to you. You know each and every heart, her needs, her wants, and her desires. If those are things of the world and not things of you, please continue to guide her in your direction until she comes to a place of full surrender to you. Show her that she can become a God fearing Proverbs 31 woman through Your grace and Your mercy. Wrap Your arms around her and love her with the agape love that only You can provide. In Your Heavenly and Most Holy Name I pray - Amen

Made in the USA
Coppell, TX
09 January 2024

27477744R10048